S0-AXQ-270

THE MINDFULNESS JOURNAL
FOR ANXIETY

The
Mindfulness
Journal
for Anxiety

DAILY PROMPTS AND PRACTICES
TO FIND PEACE

Tanya J. Peterson, MS, NCC

ALTHEA
PRESS

Copyright © 2018 by Althea Press, Emeryville, California

No part of this publication may be reproduced, stored in a retrieval system, or trans-
mitted in any form or by any means, electronic, mechanical, photocopying, recording,
scanning, or otherwise, except as permitted under Sections 107 or 108 of the 1976 United
States Copyright Act, without the prior written permission of the Publisher. Requests
to the Publisher for permission should be addressed to the Permissions Department,
Althea Press, 6005 Shellmound Street, Suite 175, Emeryville, CA 94608.

Limit of Liability/Disclaimer of Warranty: The Publisher and the author make no repre-
sentations or warranties with respect to the accuracy or completeness of the contents of
this work and specifically disclaim all warranties, including without limitation warranties
of fitness for a particular purpose. No warranty may be created or extended by sales or
promotional materials. The advice and strategies contained herein may not be suitable
for every situation. This work is sold with the understanding that the Publisher is not
engaged in rendering medical, legal, or other professional advice or services. If professional assistance is required, the services of a competent professional person should be
sought. Neither the Publisher nor the author shall be liable for damages arising here-
from. The fact that an individual, organization, or website is referred to in this work as a
citation and/or potential source of further information does not mean that the author
or the Publisher endorses the information the individual, organization, or website may
provide or recommendations they/it may make. Further, readers should be aware that
Internet websites listed in this work may have changed or disappeared between when
this work was written and when it is read.

For general information on our other products and services or to obtain technical
support, please contact our Customer Care Department within the United States at
(866) 744-2665, or outside the United States at (510) 253-0500.

Althea Press publishes its books in a variety of electronic and print formats. Some
content that appears in print may not be available in electronic books, and vice versa.

TRADEMARKS: Althea Press and the Althea Press logo are trademarks or registered
trademarks of Callisto Media Inc. and/or its affiliates, in the United States and other
countries, and may not be used without written permission. All other trademarks are the
property of their respective owners. Althea Press is not associated with any product or
vendor mentioned in this book.

Interior Designer: Liz Cosgrove
Cover Designer: Amy King
Editor: Melissa Valentine
Production Editor: Andrew Yackira
Cover and interior illustration © 2018 Monica Ramos except pp 119 and 128;
© Liliia Rudchenko/Creative Market p 119; © OpiaDesigns/Creative Market p 128

ISBN: Print 978-1-64152-306-6

THIS JOURNAL BELONGS TO:

_____

You can't stop the waves,
but you can learn to surf.

— JON KABAT-ZINN

INTRODUCTION

Life is a river. Sometimes it flows freely. It bubbles joyfully. It can be turbulent at times, churning with a strong current. It can also be clear, calm, and smooth.

Think about the choppy waters as your anxious thoughts, worries, and fears. If you're like the rest of us, you probably tend to struggle in these places—grasping and treading water, unable to flow forward. It's a normal reaction to try to control the current. But the truth is, anxiety can't be controlled any more than a river can. It will run its course, despite your best efforts. The more you try to control it, the more exhausted you'll become.

You can't control anxiety. But you can develop a new way of being so that anxiety doesn't cause you to suffer. You can do this with mindfulness. Mindfulness is how you float in the river; how you glide with the current without being carried away or pulled under.

Mindfulness is a way of experiencing your world, yourself, and your anxiety. It allows you to use all of your senses to pull your thoughts and emotions into the present moment. You'll pay attention on purpose to what is around you right now rather than remaining stuck in your thoughts, ruminating about the past or worrying about the future.

This journal is a way to begin a rewarding journey to stillness and self-discovery through mindfulness. As a National Certified Counselor, I've worked with people of all ages and backgrounds. One thing almost all people have in common is anxiety—and the desire to live free from it. I wrote this journal to show that it's possible to create yourself anew and live peacefully, not bothered by anxiety. I'm living proof of this! The prompts and exercises that follow are based on my professional knowledge, research, and personal experience.

Throughout *The Mindfulness Journal for Anxiety*, you'll explore your anxious thoughts and emotions. Writing will help you organize your thoughts and give them a bit of structure. You'll get anxiety out of your head and onto paper. In the process, you'll develop insight, awareness, meaning, and acceptance. Journaling can be a powerful healer and a master teacher. And while this book is not a cure for anxiety or replacement for other anxiety treatments, it will help you cultivate well-being in the face of anxious thoughts.

Are you ready to embrace mindfulness and begin letting go of anxiety? Take a deep breath, grab your favorite pen, and dive in.

Rivers know this:
There is no hurry. We shall get
there some day.

— A. A. MILNE

THOUGHTS WILL THINK THEMSELVES— THEY DON'T NEED ANY HELP FROM YOU

From the moment you're born, your brain automatically starts whirring. It begins to take in information and instinctively check for danger. This survival mechanism establishes a thought pattern of *looking* for problems. This can lead to anxiety throughout your life.

I want you to remember that this thought pattern is largely out of your control. It's not your fault. It's just your brain trying to keep you safe. Mindfulness teaches that events, situations, and interactions aren't the source of our problems. Instead, it's the *tangling with our thoughts* about them that causes the problem.

The following reflections and exercises will help you use mindfulness to explore and develop new perspectives on your thoughts and how they affect your well-being.

The primary cause of unhappiness is never the situation but your thoughts about it.

— ECKHART TOLLE

Thoughts aren't facts

Take a moment to consider a situation that's causing you worry and anxiety right now. What is the situation? Write the practical details below. For example: *I still have student loans to pay off.*

What are your thoughts about the situation? Scribble every worry, thought, or fear that arises when you think about this situation. For example: *I'm scared I won't be able to pay this debt. I worry this makes me an irresponsible person. Everyone else seems to be more responsible than I am. What's wrong with me?!*

Take a look at what you wrote. Notice the difference between the actual situation and the thoughts you have about it. Reflect on the differences here.

When you're alone with your thoughts, what do those thoughts say?
Tune in to your thoughts right now. Write down everything you think
without censoring it.

Pick one of the most bothersome thoughts you wrote. Imagine ignoring it. What would happen if you didn't pay attention to this thought? How would you feel?

Play with the possibilities

Write down at least four things you're worrying about. Next to each one, brainstorm alternatives. For instance, if you're worried that you said the wrong thing and now everyone hates you, think of other possibilities. Maybe no one noticed, or they agreed with you, or they'll get over it and they don't hate you. When you're finished, look over your lists. Do you know, with absolute certainty, that any of the possibilities, including your original, are accurate? Do this any time you find yourself obsessing over worries and fears.

WORRY

OTHER POSSIBILITIES

Don't believe everything you think. Thoughts are just that—thoughts.

— ALLAN LOKOS

Get to know your anxiety

Call to mind a recent time when you experienced anxiety. What was the sensation like in your mind? What set it off? Did you feel anxiety anywhere in your body? Describe it in detail below.

Imagine you're at the store, and you see your neighbor. As she approaches you, you greet her with a cheery "Hello!" She greets you, mutters something about being in a hurry, and keeps going. What's the most likely thing to immediately pop into your mind?

a) She hates me. What do I do when I see her again? I'll avoid her.

b) What did I do wrong? Was my greeting too peppy? I'm so annoying.

c) She's in a hurry.

d) What if everyone in the neighborhood hates me, too?

If you answered "c," you are already on the mindful path. You are connecting with the present moment without layering your own fears, perceptions, and assumptions onto the situation. You accept her answer and flow on with your day free of anxious thoughts.

Choices "a," "b," and "d" are products of automatic thoughts that can contribute to anxiety and, often, misery. It's part of human nature to assume the worst, but remember that assumptions aren't facts. Mindfulness is a state of being that involves simply noticing what is without making judgments.

Nothing can harm you
as much as your own thoughts
unguarded.

— THE BUDDHA

Write about a recent situation when you assumed the worst. Try to reframe the moment by accepting the reality of the situation free of judgment. What do you feel as you look at the situation in a new light?

Our thoughts can become our own worst enemy. If we let them have free rein to run amok through our mind, the result is mental chaos, worry, and anxiety. Thoughts wreak havoc, and havoc reeks! What have you tried in the past to try to rein in your thoughts? List them below—even those methods that may not be the healthiest—and reflect on how well they worked or if they didn't work.

Rate your anxiety on a scale from 1 to 10, with 1 representing very low and 10 representing the worst anxiety imaginable. Why did you pick this number? In a perfect world, what would it take to move your anxiety down the scale just one point? What is one thing you can do today to help you get lower on the scale?

1   2   3   4   5   6   7   8   9   10

Chances are, many of the things you've tried have involved focusing on your anxious thoughts or feelings—obsessing about them in order to try to "solve" them or find answers. Typically, this approach only heightens anxiety. What do you think would happen to your anxiety and worries if you just accepted them? As you reflect on this, write down the possible outcomes you envision: the negative, the positive, and all the things in between.

Open the window of your mind. Allow the fresh air, new lights, and new truths to enter.

— AMIT RAY

Open your window

Sit in a comfortable, quiet place where you can be still. Close your eyes and picture your mind with a window. The window is closed, keeping all your anxious, negative thoughts trapped inside. Gently open your window and let those anxieties escape. Watch them float away.

Sit with your open window for several minutes, or longer if you can. Your worries will likely return through the open window. That's fine. Just leave the window open for them to blow in and back out again. How does this feel? What fresh possibilities are breezing in and taking their place? Draw or write them below.

It may seem counterintuitive, but accepting anxiety doesn't mean allowing it to stick around and ruin your life. It's quite the opposite. When you accept your anxieties, you disengage and shift your focus elsewhere. The only thing you have to accept about anxious thoughts is that they are happening. You don't need to give them any more meaning than that. To practice shifting your attention away from your anxieties, choose an object near you and write down everything you observe. What does it look like? Feel like? Does it make a sound?

Observing with your senses is a fundamental part of mindfulness. Check in with yourself—do you feel more connected to the present moment? Did your anxious thoughts quiet down while observing the object? Do the exercise again with a new object. Try to notice even more qualities. You can do this exercise any time anxious thoughts flare up.

Mindfulness means being fully aware of the moment you're in instead of getting caught up in your thoughts. Living in the present keeps you away from the past and out of the future. Mindfulness is every moment. Below, make a list of times, such as stopping at a red light, when you can come into the present moment. Practice this as often as you can throughout your day. Gradually allow mindfulness to be your default instead of worry.

The sense of touch can be particularly calming and centering. Focusing on tactile sensations places your mind in the here and now. Here are some simple ways you can do this. Check anything you feel comfortable doing and try them throughout your week.

☐ Keep a rubber band around your wrist and gently snap it when your thoughts start running wild.

☐ Remove your shoes and socks and feel the ground or floor beneath your feet, focusing on the sensations of the surface.

☐ Carry a small object in your pocket or purse. When anxiety arises, hold the object and notice what it feels like in your palm or as you move it around with your fingers.

☐ Reach out and notice the temperature of objects, such as your water glass or a mug of hot coffee.

☐ When grocery shopping, concentrate on the weight and feel of each item as you add it to your basket or shopping cart.

Can you think of other ways you can use touch to keep your attention in the present moment? Maybe you have a beloved furry friend you can pet? Jot down your ideas here and come back to them often.

What is causing you anxiety right now, in this moment? Write down everything you are thinking, assuming, and worrying about.

When you become aware of your anxious thoughts, you can choose to fight with them, or to turn your attention to other things. Once you've released all your anxious thoughts onto the page, grow mindful of the room you're sitting in and the sights, sounds, smells, and tactile sensations you notice. Draw the room below, including as many details as you can. As you do this, notice as the anxiety recedes to the background of your mind.

How would your life be different if you weren't worried and anxious?

Breathing exercise

Breathe in slowly through the nose. Hold for a second or two. Exhale slowly through the mouth. Make your exhale longer than your inhale. Feel the air moving in and out of your body. Feel your diaphragm expand. Visualize your brain bathed in clean air. Do this frequently.

I'm having the thought that . . .

Remove yourself from your thoughts by noticing them and, rather than believing them and sticking to them, say, "I'm having the thought that _____." This way, "I'm a failure" becomes "I'm having the thought that I'm a failure." Try this now by listing and labeling your thoughts below. You might start to see how outlandish your thoughts can be!

Let go of the battle. Breathe quietly and let it be. Let your body relax and your heart soften. Open to whatever you experience without fighting.

— JACK KORNFIELD

INVITING
ANXIETY
IN
FOR TEA

A liberating truth: You can't make anxiety go away. If you've been struggling against anxiety, I'm here to tell you that you can finally put that fight to rest. When we accept anxiety as just part of the human experience, we can live fully in the present moment, enjoying what's happening now. This is the heart of mindfulness.

It can be difficult to accept anxiety, the very thing that is causing you so much misery! These reflections will take you to a deeper understanding of your relationship with anxiety and make room for acceptance and healing.

You must be completely awake in
the present to enjoy the tea.

— THÍCH NHẤT HẠNH

Watch your anxiety drift away

Settle into a comfortable position and place. Close your eyes and allow your anxious thoughts to come. Don't force yourself to worry, but don't try and stop anxiety, either. Visualize the thoughts drifting by on fluffy clouds or floating lazily down a river. Watch them pass by without judging or tangling with them. Breathe deeply as you do this.

What would you rather have: a life without anxiety, or a life without joy?

Why do you have to choose?

Close your eyes for a moment and consider what it would be like to stop fighting anxiety and allow it to be a part of your life. On a scale from 1 to 10, with 10 being the worst fear imaginable, how much do you fear this?

1   2   3   4   5   6   7   8   9   10

Below, write about how this makes you feel mentally and physically.

How willing are you right now to invite anxiety in for tea?

a) Not at all. Anxiety can make its own tea and drink it somewhere else.

b) Ugh, do I have to? Anxiety will just talk the whole time and spoil all the fun.

c) I don't like the idea, but I'm willing to explore it on the off chance that it might work.

d) Yes! Bring in anxiety. I hope it's thirsty!

Reflect on your response to the above question. Without judging it or yourself, explore the reasons for your answer. What makes you willing to accept your anxiety or what is holding you back?

Focusing on anxiety when you're trying to enjoy life is much like (check all that apply):

☐ Charging through a six-foot spiderweb and stopping to clean it off before continuing where you were going

☐ Applying sunscreen at the beach just before the wind picks up and blasts you with sand that sticks to you for the rest of the day

☐ Tossing the contents of a large container of glitter into a fan and commanding yourself to pick up every piece by hand before you can go to the party

☐ Running toward a finish line that keeps getting farther away

☐ Riding a merry-go-round that won't stop (and has ugly, uncomfortable seats)

In my experience, anxiety can be like any of those things depending on the situation and your own thought patterns. Think for a moment about these scenarios and how you could change them—for instance, by hopping off the merry-go-round or leaving the glitter to clean up a bit later. Anxiety works the same way.

Let it RAIN

Used by mindfulness leader Tara Brach and adapted from Michele McDonald, RAIN is an acronym for a powerful mindfulness exercise. When you find yourself fighting with anxiety rather than accepting it, get back to your present moment with this practice:

Recognize your anxious thoughts and feelings.

Allow, or accept, your anxiety to simply be there.

Investigate without judging: what's happening to make anxiety strong right now?

Natural awareness through mindfulness: use your senses to ground yourself in the moment and relax in your awareness.

Consider what you most want. What is preventing you from having it or working toward it?

What would it be like if I could accept life—accept this moment—exactly as it is?

— TARA BRACH

Affirm it to make it so

Affirmations are a great way to focus on exactly what you want. If you create a statement to affirm what you want, it offers an antidote for whatever is in the way or scares you. For example, if you constantly feel overwhelmed and don't know how you can handle everything, a good affirmation might be: *I can handle anything that comes my way.*

   In the space below, write the top 10 things that are causing you anxiety. Then, next to each one, write an affirmation, or antidote statement. Repeat an affirmation to yourself whenever you need one.

ANXIOUS FEELING   AFFIRMATION/ANTIDOTE STATEMENT

I spy

This game focuses your attention on what is happening now. When you catch yourself caught up in anxiety, tell yourself, "I spy with my little eye . . . " and begin to mentally list everything you see. Be descriptive. Do you see a tree, or do you see a tall maple tree with green leaves waving in a gentle breeze with roots protruding from the earth? What is the bark like? Are there bugs, birds, squirrels, seed pods?

Now, rather than fighting with anxiety, you have immersed yourself fully in your present moment!

Anxiety is part of life. Describe a recent situation in which anxiety occupied you and took away your enjoyment. What was the event (a trip to the store, a concert, relaxing at home)? Who was with you? What was on your mind? In what ways did anxiety ruin your time?

What could you have focused on then instead of anxiety? List as many things as you can, no matter how small they might seem. Reflect on how the memory of this moment would be different had you shifted your focus at the time.

A big part of acceptance is allowing something to be present without judging it as good or bad. Anxiety feels bad when we get caught up in it. In reality, anxiety just is. It's a bunch of random thoughts. If you stop viewing anxiety as bad, what would happen? How would this perspective change your relationship with anxiety? What would change, and how?

One is a great deal less anxious
if one feels perfectly free
to be anxious, and the same may
be said of guilt.

— ALAN W. WATTS

Acceptance does not mean giving up or giving in. Acceptance means leaving anxiety alone and turning your attention to the quality of life you want. When you accept anxiety, it has less power over you, not more. Finish this promise: *By accepting anxiety, I will be able to . . .*

When you accept anxiety's presence in your life, you free yourself to do anything other than tangle with anxiety. Begin a running list of people, events, situations, and places that can now be enjoyed even though anxiety is hanging around.

Non-judgment quiets the internal dialogue, and this opens once again the doorway to creativity.

— DEEPAK CHOPRA

When your mind is full of the present moment rather than cluttered with worries and what-ifs, you have room to create yourself. In the space below, brainstorm ideas you have for your ideal self. Who will you create?

Body scan

Anxiety has physical symptoms, such as tightness and tension, but you can't take care of them if you're distracted. A body scan is a mindfulness tool to help bring you back into your body so you can identify and release any anxiety you're feeling.

Get comfortable and turn your attention to your toes. Wiggle them. How do they feel? Are they holding tension? If so, move them around and breathe in deeply, visualizing fresh air bathing your toes. Continue scanning slowly and deliberately until you reach the top of your head. Notice the effects of anxiety and nurture them with attention and love, but otherwise let anxiety be. Notice how your mind feels calmer after scanning your body. You're fully present.

A mindful cup of tea

Make a fresh cup of hot tea. Choose a comfortable, quiet place where you can sit and savor the experience of your tea. Concentrate on the taste, appearance, temperature, and aroma. Feel the warmth pass down your throat. When your mind begins to worry, don't try to force it away. Just turn your attention back to your tea with a smile.

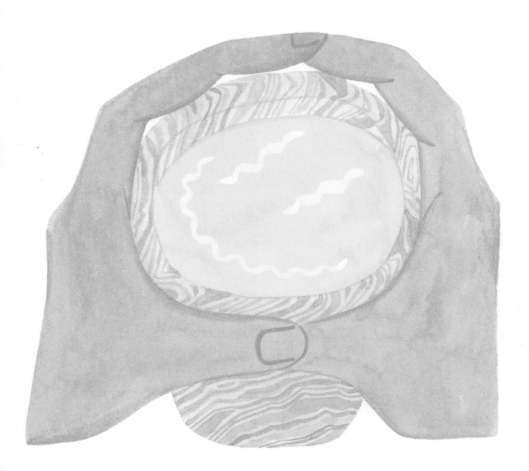

Tea is an act complete in its simplicity. When I drink tea, there is only me and the tea. The rest of the world dissolves.

— THÍCH NHẤT HẠNH

THE
PERSON
UNDERNEATH
THE
ANXIETY

Repeat after me: I am not my anxiety. I know sometimes this is hard to believe because anxiety can be so all consuming. But there's a big difference in believing, "I am anxious," versus "I have anxiety." The first one implies that anxiety is who you are, while the second one means that anxiety is merely something you experience, like hunger or thirst.

When you separate yourself from your anxiety, you remove it from your identity and it becomes less personal. Doing this allows you to turn away from anxiety and instead reflect on your true self—the self that lives underneath your worries and anxieties.

Meditation practice isn't about
trying to throw ourselves away
and become something better.
It's about befriending
who we are already.

— PEMA CHÖDRÖN

Be your own best friend

The meaning underlying Pema Chödrön's words on the previous page is very powerful. You don't have to replace yourself with something better. You are wonderful and unique just as you are. Nothing, including anxiety, changes that. Take some time to reflect on your positive qualities. Describe yourself below as if you were your own best friend. Be sure to give yourself lots of love and compliments!

Part of who you are is made up by the roles you play in life. From what you do for work (whether it's paid or unpaid) to your relationships and responsibilities, list your roles below. (For example, you might write, "I am a mother.")

Roles are very important, but they tend to be defined in relation to other people. An important step in loving yourself is realizing that you are more than your place among others. Your true essence exists in the quiet within you. Be still with yourself for several moments. Breathe slowly and deeply. Who are you at your core? What's been true about you since you were a child? What are your values, interests, passions, dreams? Describe them below, focusing on yourself rather than the roles you play.

Developing awareness

This is a mindfulness meditation in which you become still and simply observe. Set a timer to sound gently after five minutes. Each time you do this, you can increase the meditation duration by one or two minutes.

Close your eyes, and breathe deeply. Concentrate on the feel of the air moving in and out of your body and the sound of it coming and going, too. Notice any thoughts you have, but don't judge them, fight with them, or stick to them. Notice them, then let them drift away. Notice sounds, smells, and physical sensations. When the timer sounds, gently open your eyes, take a deep breath, and smile softly.

Write about the experience. What was it like to do this? Joyful? Frustrating? Was your mind noisy or quiet? Did the exercise change your relationship with anxiety? How?

What are your gifts? What are you good at? What can you do that no one else can? Describe your unique gifts and talents.

_____

_____

_____

_____

_____

_____

_____

_____

_____

_____

_____

_____

_____

_____

_____

_____

_____

How easy was it for you to write about your own gifts and strengths? Did any anxiety creep in as you wrote about this? Notice these thoughts and then let them go. Acknowledge that anxiety about expressing your talents doesn't change the fact that you have them! Tune into what's true about your gifts and try to release any overana-lyzing. Part of mindfulness is accepting ourselves for who we are.

Mindfulness is a way of befriending ourselves and our experience.

— JON KABAT-ZINN

Self, meet Me

Mindfully introduce yourself—to yourself. Stand in front
of a mirror, introduce yourself, and state your character
strengths, passions, values and how you use them to live
well and move forward. Introduce yourself as a master in
accepting your anxiety.

Write about your true purpose in life.

What scares you the most?

How are fear and anxiety holding you back from your purpose and living your best life?

Stand up to your anxiety

Anxiety doesn't have to hold you back anymore! Write anxiety a letter giving it a piece of your mind. What holes exist in its stories? What is wrong with it? How are things going to be different now? How are you moving forward?

DEAR ANXIETY,

SINCERELY,

Close your eyes and visualize your mind. What do you see? What is it saying? If you could touch it, would it be sharp or sticky or rough or smooth or something else? Describe your mind.

Much of spiritual life is
self-acceptance, maybe all of it.

— JACK KORNFIELD

Now close your eyes and be mindful of your heart. Describe your heart, how it looks and feels. What are the tender spots? The areas filled with warmth and goodness? Sadness? Is it soft, hard, or prickly?

Spiritual life refers to (circle all that apply):

Religion

Belief in a higher power

Having a sense of meaning

Connection to something "bigger"

Living true to your values and beliefs

Worshiping in a church, synagogue, mosque, temple, home, or outdoors

Feeling gratitude

Living with lovingkindness for yourself and others

If you circled all of the choices, you're right. If you circled only a few that resonated with you, you're also right. If you circled none of them but thought of your own, you're still right. Spiritual life is deeply personal.

Describe your own sense of spirituality. The more we understand about our beliefs, the more we can accept ourselves and love ourselves.

Draw out your breath

René Descartes, the 17th-century French philosopher, proclaimed, "I think, therefore I am." Thoughts, though, don't prove or define our existence (and, as we know, they can cause us a whole lot of trouble, including anxiety). Instead, our breath is proof of our existence. You breathe, therefore you are.

Breathe slowly and deeply, in through your nose and out through your mouth. Let your breath settle into a relaxed rhythm. Listen to the air move in and out, and notice how breathing feels throughout your body. Now, draw out your breath—literally. Use the space provided to doodle as you breathe. Simply move your pencil to the rhythm of your breath. Watch, detached, as your hand moves about the page. Pay attention to your breath and your pencil, and let your breath blow your thoughts away.

Five things

Write down:

Five things that are causing you anxiety right now:

1. ....
2. ....
3. ....
4. ....
5. ....

Five things that are on your mind that you can control, and how you will take charge of them:

1. ....
2. ....
3. ....
4. ....
5. ....

Five things that are on your mind but are out of your control, and how you will accept them and move forward:

1. ....
2. ....
3. ....
4. ....
5. ....

Five actions you can take this week to create joy and well-being:

1. _____
2. _____
3. _____
4. _____
5. _____

Five things you appreciate about yourself today, regardless of your current worries and stresses:

1. _____
2. _____
3. _____
4. _____
5. _____

Imagine waking up in the morning and your anxiety was magically, completely gone. What would your day look like? How would your life and your relationship with yourself be different?

Hands-on meditation

Touch and sound are powerful senses that can ground you in the moment. Sit in a comfortable and quiet meditation spot. Turn on music according to what mood you want to cultivate: energetic, calm, inspired, reflective, or any other emotion that's calling to you. Place a tray of sand or a bowl of uncooked rice in front of you. Listen to the music and use your fingers to play with the rice or sand. Feel your stress melt away as you pay attention to how the music sounds and how the sand or rice feels as you gently move it around.

TIP: Build a playlist on your phone, tablet, or computer so you'll have it on hand whenever you want to do this hands-on meditation. Do it often!

You are the sky.
Everything else is just
the weather.

— PEMA CHÖDRÖN

The past is done. The future has yet to happen. Your life is now. What is within you in this moment is who you are—nothing else. Draw symbols or pictures to represent your contentment in the present.

What lies behind us and what lies before us are tiny matters compared to what lies within us.

— HENRY STANLEY HASKINS

THE
MINDFUL
WAY

The power and the beauty of mindfulness is that it isn't just a tool for a life well lived. Mindfulness *is* life well lived. Sure, mindfulness is a means to let go of anxiety, but as you practice it, it quietly becomes a way of being.

Let the following activities guide you along your mindfulness path.

We are awakened to the
profound realization
that the true path to
liberation is to let go
of everything.

— JACK KORNFIELD

The things we do on a daily basis are great starting points for incorporating mindfulness into our everyday life. List 10 things in your daily routine that you can start paying attention to instead of anxiety. This can be as simple as mindfully feeling the warm water on your hands as you wash the dishes. Small moments matter!

1.

2.

3.

4.

5.

6.

7.

8.

9.

10.

Turn grumbles into gratitude

Life isn't perfect. It's okay to grumble about things on occasion. But instead of being consumed by the negative, the next time you catch yourself grumbling, immediately shift your focus. For every grumble, jot down two things for which you're grateful. Try it now. What has been negative today? What else is going on that you're grateful for? Do this any time negativity bubbles up!

Tune into your vision

Struggling with anxiety keeps you locked in conflict, and you end up fusing with what you don't want: stress and anxiety. Once you let go of the struggle, you can shift your attention to what you want instead of anxiety.

A great way to do this is to create a vision board. Gather images and quotations that highlight your vision for your life. Imagine yourself being exactly the "you" you want to be, from your job to where you live to how you spend your time to what you believe. Use drawings, words, phrases, pictures, and magazine cutouts to depict your ideal self. Start your vision board right here in this journal, and then take it off the pages and onto your wall. Use it as a visual reminder of everything you want to be despite anxiety.

Mindfulness is about being
fully awake in our lives. It is
about perceiving the exquisite
vividness of each moment. We also
gain immediate access to our own
powerful inner resources
for insight, transformation,
and healing.

— JON KABAT-ZINN

Why do you want to be fully awake in your life? What are some things you're excited to be more present for?

Appreciate beauty and let yourself experience awe. Awe takes us out of our thoughts and inspires humble appreciation for the world. Seek out something that invokes awe—this can be natural beauty, such as the ocean or a sweeping vista, a work of art in a museum or art book, or a beautiful building in your town or city. Draw or describe the experience below using your senses. Capture the feeling of awe.

Let your heart fill with wonder

Make a list of 5–10 places in your town that inspire awe and wonder, and go on a scavenger hunt. Visit them one at a time and see them in a new way.

1.

2.

3.

4.

5.

6.

7.

8.

9.

10.

The good life box

Decorate a shoebox or large jar. Make it uniquely you. Place strips of paper and a pen near the box. Record things you've noticed about the world around you, your own anxiety levels, your building sense of calm, or things you're grateful for. Keep the strips in the box until it's full, then read them and enjoy the reminders. List five things you'd put in the jar right now.

1.
2.
3.
4.
5.

What is important to you? How can you pay more attention to what's more important than anxiety?

When you become aware that anxiety is taking over your day, instead you could:

a) Retreat into bed.

b) Argue with your anxious thoughts.

c) Accept your anxious thoughts.

d) Pay attention to your life in the moment.

You may want to do two of these options, and perhaps you have done them in the past. Cross those two out. The other two are the healthy choices that shift your attention from what you don't want onto what you do what. Circle those two.

Did you cross out "a" and "b" and circle "c" and "d"? If so, congratulations. You're well on your way to living mindfully.

Light as a feather

Living mindfully can make you feel lighter. Use this exercise to remember to float on a breeze rather than struggle against the wind. Lie on your back with a supply of feathers beside you. (You can buy them in craft stores or pluck them off feather dusters.) Place a feather on your lips, and then gently blow it into the air. See how many times you can do this before losing the feather. Now, record what things looked like from on your back: what the feather felt like on your lips, the appearance of the feather as it floated in the air, any sounds in the room, the feel of your chest rising and falling, and anything else you noticed during this mindfulness exercise.

In today's rush, we all think too much, seek too much, want too much, and forget about the joy of just being.

— ECKHART TOLLE

What does the "joy of just being" mean to you?
  Describe or draw it here.

On a scale from 1 to 10, with 1 meaning not at all and 10 representing absolute harmony, how balanced is your life right now?

1   2   3   4   5   6   7   8   9   10

In what ways do you feel off-kilter? What do you need in order to restore balance?

_____

_____

_____

_____

_____

_____

_____

_____

_____

_____

_____

_____

_____

_____

_____

_____

Good enough

Look for the good in your life—not the perfect. Unrealistic expectations and a need for perfection can trigger high anxiety. Practice shifting your perspective so you are increasingly happy with "good" and "good enough." Draw a picture of someone you love, a garden, a pet, or anything you want to draw. Draw it here using your nondominant hand. When you're done, reflect on how you feel about it and try and appreciate things you like about your "imperfect" artwork.

Start a collection of things that remind you of peace and calm. What might you collect? Pebbles? Shells? Feathers? Quotes? Brainstorm and sketch some ideas here:

This list contains some examples of mindfulness activities. Put a check mark by any that you are willing to try. Place question marks by those that you're unsure about. Circle three that you are excited to try right away. Feel free to add your own ideas inspired by the exercises you've done so far in this book.

- [ ] Set a timer to remind you to stop and take 10 slow, deep breaths every hour.

- [ ] Slowly walk barefoot through the grass. Notice how the individual blades feel against your feet.

- [ ] Put on music you love, and scribble and doodle to the beat.

- [ ] Sculpt with clay or Play-Doh. Pay attention to how it feels in your hands, squishing between your fingers. Create forms and start over, reflecting on the impermanence of everything.

- [ ] Prepare a meal mindfully, activating all your senses as you add each ingredient and combine different flavors.

- [ ] Replace 30 minutes of daily screen time (TV, computer, phone) with an activity or hobby you truly enjoy doing. Work up to an hour or more!

- [ ] Take a slow walk with no particular destination in mind. Leave your phone at home! Appreciate the beauty around you (even if it's not immediately obvious) as you take in the sights, sounds, and scents.

- [ ] Embrace your inner child and buy some bubbles. As you blow the bubbles, feel your diaphragm expanding and contracting. Vary the strength of your breath to make bubbles of different sizes. Observe how they float in the air and dance in the light.